Let's look at
the Portraits of Archimboldo

Created by
Claude Delafosse
and Gallimard Jeunesse

At the back of this book
you will find a press-out paper torch,
and a pocket to keep it in.

FIRST DISCOVERY / TORCHLIGHT
MOONLIGHT PUBLISHING

Come into the imaginary world of a most unusual painter, Giuseppe Archimboldo, and discover his amazing creations.

In this book you are able to look at the countless details and brilliant colours of his paintings.

Thanks to a simple torch made of paper, you can explore the dark pages of this book.
It's like magic!

You'll find the torch on the last page.
Press it out and slide it between the plastic
page and the black page underneath it. You'll
be amazed by what you light up!

As you move it around,
little by little you'll discover
all the details hidden in each picture.

Giuseppe Archimboldo was a painter who lived during the Italian Renaissance.

He was born in Milan in 1527 and spent a large part of his life at the courts in Vienna and Prague.
He painted most original portraits by placing objects next to one another to form a face.

Still life paintings which are very much alive!

The fruit, vegetables, flowers, shells... of Archimboldo have come down to us through the centuries in all their original brilliance.

Spring

A head made of flowers, a body all

of leaves, a collar of daisies.

that's Archimboldo's Spring.

Can you spot the little bell-like flowers

of the lily of the valley in

this magnificent bouquet?

Summer

A courgette for a nose,

a peach for a cheek,

cherries for lips,

a pear for a chin; that is how

Archimboldo paints the

portrait of Summer.

Can you find the ears of corn?

Autumn

A pear nose,

an apple cheek,

a sweet chestnut mouth,

an oaty beard

and curranty hair;

Archimboldo's Autumn is dressed

in an old barrel.

Can you see the snail?

Winter

A head of bark,

a mushroom mouth,

ivy for hair,

straw for clothes.

Archimboldo's Winter sends a cold

shiver down your spine. Thank

goodness for Spring!

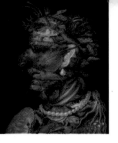

Water

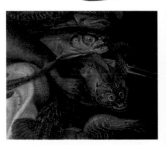

Sea-water or fresh-water,

Fish or shellfish...

Archimboldo portrays water with

an unbelievable mixture of every

kind of water creature.

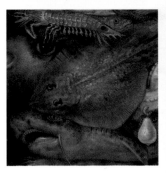

A cheek of hake, a shark

for a mouth, a crab shell for a

breast plate. Have you found the

sea horse?

The Librarian

Open books, closed books,

upright books, books leaning,

lying flat on their side or piled high,

Archimboldo has conjured up an

astonishing librarian.

And have you counted his paper

fingers?

The Vegetable Man

A radish nose,

a mushroom mouth,

hazel nuts for eyes,

an onion cheek;

such is the vegetable man

created by Archimboldo.

Can't you see him?

Turn the book upside down and

you will recognize him!

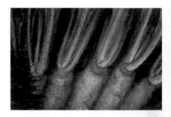

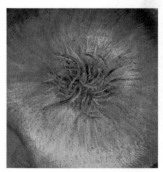

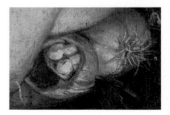

Rudolf II Glorified

Crowned with fruit,

wreathed in corn,

wearing a splendid sash

of flowers, this sumptuous

garden is sculpted

like an emperor. That is

how Archimboldo

portrays his friend,

Prince Rudolf II,

so magnificently.

These details are from the dark pages of the book.

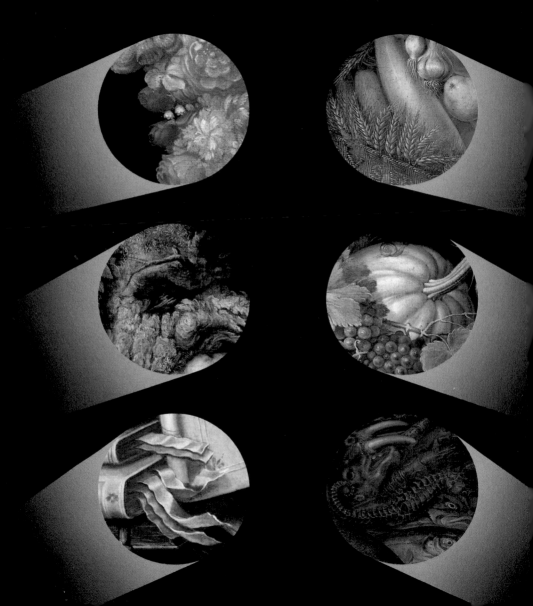

Can you find them using your magic torch?

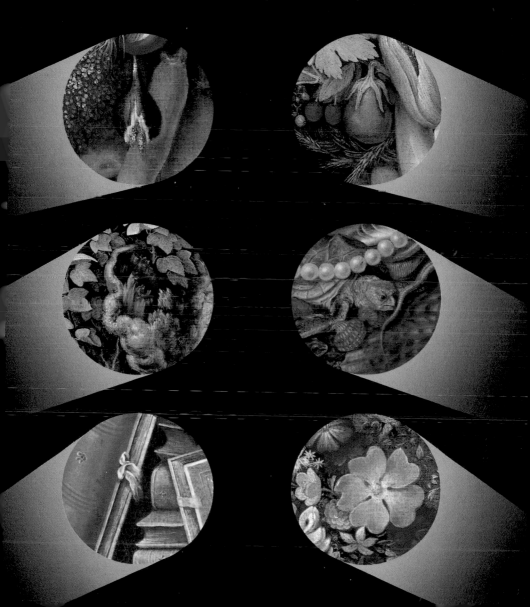

FIRST DISCOVERY: OVER 100 TITLES AVAILABLE IN FOUR SERIES

American Indians
Animal Camouflage
Animals in Danger
Babies
Bears
The Beaver
The Bee
Being Born
Birds
Boats
The Body
The Building Site
The Butterfly
The Castle
Cathedrals
Cats
Christmas and New Year
Clothes and Costumes
Colours
Counting
The Crocodile
The Desert
Dinosaurs
Dogs
Ducks
The Eagle
Earth and Sky
The Egg
The Elephant
Farm Animals
Finding a Mate*
Firefighting
Flowers
Flying
Football
The Frog
Fruit
Growing Up
Halloween
Hands, Feet and Paws

Homes
The Horse
How the Body Works
The Internet
The Jungle
The Ladybird
Light
The Lion
Monkeys and Apes
Mountains
The Mouse
Music
On Wheels
The Owl
Penguins
Pictures
Prehistoric People
Pyramids
Rabbits
The Riverbank
The Seashore
Shapes
Shops
Small Animals in the Home
Sport
The Story of Bread
The Telephone
Time
The Toolbox
Town
Trains
The Tree
Under the Ground
Up and Down
Vegetables
Water
The Weather
Whales
The Wind
The Wolf

FIRST DISCOVERY / ATLAS
Animal Atlas
Atlas of Animals in Danger
Atlas of Civilizations
Atlas of Countries
Atlas of the Earth
Atlas of France
Atlas of Islands
Atlas of Peoples
Atlas of Space
Plant Atlas

FIRST DISCOVERY / ART
Animals
Henri Matisse
The Impressionists
Landscapes
The Louvre
Pablo Picasso
Paintings
Portraits
Sculpture
Vincent van Gogh

FIRST DISCOVERY / TORCHLIGHT
Let's Look at Animals by Night
Let's Look at Animals Underground
Let's Look at Archimboldo's Portraits
Let's Look at Castles
Let's Look at Caves
Let's Look at Dinosaurs
Let's Look at Fish Underwater
Let's Look at Life below the City
Let's Look at Insects
Let's Look at the Jungle
Let's Look at the Sky
Let's Look at the Zoo by Night
Let's Look for Lost Treasure
Let's Look inside the Body
Let's Look inside Pyramids

Translator: Penelope Stanley-Baker
ISBN 1 85103 290 8
© 1999 Editions Gallimard Jeunesse
English text © 2000 by Moonlight Publishing Ltd
First published in the United Kingdom 2000
by Moonlight Publishing Limited, The King's Manor, East Hendred, Oxon. OX12 8JY
Printed in Italy by Editoriale Lloyd